But Frederick, I said,
these people are my friends!
Look at them
(That one? Long story...)
I admit, some I have not chosen,
they simply return, like delightful illnesses
Others have bombarded my soul
Such devotion, such extremes, such impossible demands
A few have even rolled around
in my juicier dreams
But tonight, Frederick, you and me
Let us not dwell on the whys and wherefores
Let us drink with them,
compliment them on their interesting garb
and pluck the feathers from a succulent bird!

# GATHERINGS

# GATHERINGS

## A YEAR OF INVITATIONS

# NATANIËL

PHOTOGRAPHS BY CLINTON LUBBE

Human & Rousseau
Cape Town  Pretoria

# Contents

# Come Over

I don't like going out, never have, never will. I travel for a living, most nights I am on the road to or from concerts, and a day off or a night at home is a blessing, an event that has to be celebrated. That means doing three of my favourite things: cooking, eating and seeing my friends.

There is always the option of going to a restaurant, but unless there is a private dining room or the chef is one of the ten best in the world or the owner is a personal friend or romantic ties with the manager are strongly suggested, it is bound to be a disappointment or a disaster.

No, I stay in and I cook. I cook for love, for peace, for fun, for hunger or prosperity, for richer or poorer, for better or worse. I cook the food that I love, that I miss, that I never had, that I saw somewhere or dream of, food that does not intimidate me or take up all my time, food that represents my life and makes my guests return time and time again. I fail and I falter, but I try to keep it natural, fresh, organic, healthy and simple.

This book is not about how to cook, but rather a documenting of gatherings, events, celebrations and magical get-togethers at my house over the course of a year. Everything was cooked, photographed and enjoyed at my house, nothing was borrowed or styled, this is how I eat. It is intended as both an inspiration and a tribute to home cooking and entertaining – practical, affordable, elegant, spontaneous, grand, relaxed, formal, informal, fun, opulent or intimate. The recipes given here are in the simplest form; feel free to add on, improvise and improve.

My great, great thanks to Clinton for taking these beautiful pictures and trusting my vision, to Lyn, the best make-up artist in the world, for the energy, the joy and the jawline, to Wess-Lee for the hours of shopping and chopping, to Ellen and Jan for cleaning up, polishing, dragging around furniture and pretending everything tasted good, to Topsi and Rachel who took hundreds of calls and answered all my questions, and to everyone who unfolded a napkin at my table over the past twelve months.

Finally, I have a life. I use self-raising flour and store-bought puff pastry, judge me if you want to.

Also, every oven is different. I use a convection oven, so temperatures in a conventional oven may need to be a few degrees higher or the baking time a few minutes longer.

Bless this food, bless this house.

Nataniël
April 2009

*Note: Unless otherwise indicated, all recipes in this book are for 6 people*

# Breakfast or Later

At the best of times I find breakfast a tough one. Juggling two careers (the hours, not the work) is not always easy, and there is seldom enough time for a decent breakfast. And if, like me, you were born without a metabolism, skipping breakfast is not an option. That leaves you with those fast and unappetising horrors like cereal, smoothies, porridge or fresh fruit. Can the day get any worse?

But on those few mornings that you have an extra hour or two and, even better, guests, breakfast can be the most glorious occasion. I cannot think of a greater joy than a beautiful setting, a steaming cup of tea, perfectly made toast and soft scrambled eggs.

Breakfast needs a crisp white tablecloth, fresh flowers, linen napkins, attractive tableware, a soft gown and some classical music. And no phones! Life is good and will get even better with food like this:

Scrambled Eggs with Green Butter

Fig and Rosemary Scones with Crispy Bacon

Apple Breakfast Pies

Morning Dessert

# Scrambled Eggs with Green Butter

## per serving

2 tbsp Green Butter

2 large eggs, lightly beaten

freshly ground black pepper (optional)

Heat butter in pan over medium heat
Pour eggs into pan
Do not stir or whisk or use a fork
Let cook until eggs just begin to set at bottom of pan
Use a spatula and slowly push through eggs
Remove pan from heat when a quarter of the eggs are still runny
Season with black pepper, if preferred
Serve immediately with toasted bread and more Green Butter

## Green Butter

1 heaped tsp fresh basil, finely chopped

2 heaped tsp fresh watercress, finely chopped

200 g butter, softened

Mix herbs into butter and refrigerate until needed

# Fig and Rosemary Scones with Crispy Bacon

2 cups self-raising flour
pinch of salt
100 g butter, cut into small cubes
1 cup buttermilk
8 soft dried figs, chopped
1 tsp fresh rosemary, finely chopped
18 narrow strips of bacon
honey

Set oven to 200 °C
Lightly grease oven tray with butter
Sift flour into mixing bowl, add salt
Use your hands to rub butter into flour
Stir in buttermilk, figs and rosemary
Place on buttered surface and roll out lightly
Use cookie cutter and cut out 12 rounds
Place on prepared oven tray
Bake for 7 minutes
Place bacon in a cool pan
Heat pan and fry until crisp on both sides
Serve with scones, drizzled with honey

# Apple Breakfast Pies

On the days that I *have* to do the fruit-and-fibre thing, this is the only
way I can get it into my body.

1¼ cup muesli

1 tbsp butter

7 Golden Delicious apples, peeled, cored and cut into slices

2 tbsp demerara sugar

3 heaped tbsp dried cranberries

1 tbsp brandy

4 tbsp water

pinch of ground cinnamon

100 g white cheddar, grated

extra demerara sugar for sprinkling on top

Set oven to 200 °C

Divide muesli between six ramekins

Melt butter in a saucepan

Add apples and sugar

Stir until apples are golden brown but still firm

Add cranberries, brandy and water, and stir until sauce thickens

Remove from heat and stir in cinnamon

Sprinkle cheese over muesli

Spoon apple and cranberry mixture on top

Sprinkle with a bit of sugar, and bake in preheated oven for 10 minutes

Serve hot

# Morning Dessert

This is so delicious you'll never think it's breakfast or good for you.

### per serving

200 ml plain yogurt

1 banana, cut into chunks

5 fresh strawberries

1 tbsp honey

½ tsp vanilla extract

handful of fresh raspberries (for topping)

Combine first five ingredients in a food processor and blend until creamy
Pour into a tall glass and top with raspberries

# Lunch, No Meat

These days I find myself preparing and eating more and more meat-free meals. Not only do I find it healthier, easier to prepare, less expensive and more colourful, but also much lighter, especially in the middle of the day when you just need to take a break and build up your strength without getting weighed down by a heavy meal. I also find that more of my friends and colleagues are willing to give vegetables a second chance, making it necessary for me to build a bigger repertoire of bloodless foods.

The following dishes are simple enough to be prepared at any time, and are also tasty and aesthetically pleasing enough to be served to guests. I've never cooked any of them the same way twice, they allow for much improvisation and many variations.

Bruschetta with White Beans and Gruyère

Mushrooms with Leeks and Sage

Fresh Tomato and Spinach Pasta

Roasted Roots, Twice Dressed

# Bruschetta with White Beans and Gruyère

1 tin (240 g) white beans, drained
zest of ½ lemon, finely grated
extra virgin olive oil (about 2 tbsp)
sea salt
freshly ground black pepper
24 cocktail tomatoes
1 tbsp vegetable oil
6 slices country bread
1 tbsp olive oil
100 g gruyère, shaved with vegetable peeler
fresh watercress
Lemon and Thyme Syrup

Set oven to 180 °C
In a mixing bowl, mash beans lightly
with a fork
(Texture should be lumpy)
Stir in lemon zest and 1 tsp olive oil
Season with salt and pepper, cover and
set aside
Toss tomatoes with vegetable oil and
place on an oven tray
Roast in oven for about 20 minutes
(Cooking time varies with size and
ripeness of tomatoes)
Fry bread on both sides in a very hot
griddle pan
Remove from heat and brush each
slice lightly on one side with olive oil
Spoon bean paste onto each slice, and
top with tomatoes
Arrange gruyère shavings over
tomatoes, and garnish with watercress
Drizzle with Lemon and Thyme Syrup

## Lemon and Thyme Syrup

½ cup sugar
juice of 3 lemons
¾ cup water
3 sprigs fresh thyme

Combine ingredients in a saucepan
Bring to the boil
Lower heat and let simmer for
5 minutes
Allow to cool and remove thyme

# Mushrooms with Leeks and Sage

1 tbsp butter
2 cups chopped leeks
12 giant brown mushrooms
50 g mixed nuts, finely chopped
12 fresh sage leaves
12 round slices of mozzarella (slightly smaller than mushrooms)
sea salt
freshly ground black pepper

Set oven to 180 °C
Heat butter in a saucepan
Add leeks and let sweat over very low heat for about 1 hour
Clean mushrooms with a brush or a cloth and remove stems
Arrange them, bottom-side up, on one or two baking sheets
Spoon some leeks into the centre of each mushroom
Sprinkle with nuts
Place a sage leaf on top of each mushroom
Top with cheese rounds
Bake in preheated oven until cheese has melted and starts to brown
Season with salt and black pepper, and serve with fresh bread and salad

# Fresh Tomato and Spinach Pasta

1 tbsp vegetable oil
2 cloves garlic, chopped
600 g cocktail tomatoes, halved
leaves of 6 sprigs of thyme
1 tsp sugar
½ cup water
1 tbsp tomato paste
500 g uncooked penne pasta
200 g fresh baby spinach leaves
sea salt
freshly ground black pepper
parmesan

Heat oil in a saucepan
Add garlic and stir for 1 minute
Add 400 g of the tomatoes, thyme, sugar, water and tomato paste
Bring to the boil and cook for 10 minutes
Keep warm
Cook pasta in lightly salted water until al dente
Drain and stir in the sauce
Add remaining tomatoes and spinach
Cook and stir until spinach has wilted
Season with salt and pepper
Spoon into a serving dish or individual pasta bowls
Grate parmesan over and serve immediately

# Roasted Roots, Twice Dressed

400 g sweet potatoes
400 g parsnips
400 g baby carrots
3 large onions
2 tbsp vegetable oil
500 g potatoes
sea salt
freshly ground black pepper
Lemon Dressing
Herbed Crème Fraîche
fresh herbs for garnishing

Set oven to 180 °C
Peel sweet potatoes and parsnips,
rinse and dry
Cut into chunks similar in size
to baby carrots
Peel and quarter onions
Arrange these vegetables on an
oven tray
Drizzle with 1 tbsp oil and bake in
preheated oven for 40 minutes
Peel, wash and dry potatoes, then cut
into extremely thin strips
Place on another oven tray, drizzle
with 1 tbsp oil and bake in
same oven for 30 minutes, or
until golden brown
Remove potatoes from oven, season
with salt and pepper, and set aside
Remove root vegetables from oven and
toss with Lemon Dressing
Return to oven for 5 minutes
Remove from oven and season
with salt and pepper

Spoon vegetables in the centre of
individual plates
Top with bundles of potato strips
Spoon Herbed Crème Fraîche around
and garnish with fresh herbs

## Lemon Dressing

2 tbsp extra virgin olive oil
1 tbsp honey
juice of ½ lemon

Whisk ingredients together until
cloudy

## Herbed Crème Fraîche

180 g crème fraîche
1 tbsp finely chopped chives
1 tbsp roughly chopped flat-leaf parsley
1 tbsp finely chopped fresh thyme
pinch of salt
freshly ground black pepper

Mix first four ingredients together
Season with salt and pepper

# Valentine

Valentine's dinner is not an isolated occasion that takes place once a year on the 14th of February. No, it is a special meal you regularly serve to a loved one, a close friend or anybody who is going through a tough time and needs a little extra care.

The food of love should be light, fresh, fragrant, sensual and beautiful. Choose dishes that may be prepared ahead of time and only require last-minute baking or heating. You should spend the evening with your guest and not at the stove.

The table setting itself should be fun, bold and theatrical. Do not fall into the trap of soft pinks and faded apricots, that is how you set the table when you're leaving someone. Welcome your guest with a spectacular drink, as expensive and exotic as your time or finances will allow.

MENU

Lover's Lick

Risotto Cake

Baked Salmon with Small Beets

White Choc Cookies with Rose Cloud

# Lover's Lick

French champagne or Cap Classique
2 sheets of edible gold leaf
preserved ginger, thinly sliced (alternative option)

Pour champagne into two tall flutes
Wait until foam has settled
Use tweezers and place gold leaf on top of champagne
If gold leaf is not available, place 2 or 3 thin slices of preserved ginger in
bottom of each glass before filling with champagne

# Risotto Cake

1 tbsp butter
200 g celery, chopped
1 large onion, chopped
200 g baby spinach, chopped
1½ cups arborio rice
1 cup white wine
4 cups chicken stock
2 tbsp finely grated parmesan
3 eggs, beaten
freshly ground black pepper
extra virgin olive oil

Set oven to 180 °C
Heat butter in a pan
Add celery and onion, and sweat over low heat for 15 minutes
Add spinach and stir until wilted
Add rice and stir for 1 minute
Add wine and stir until absorbed
Add stock a little at a time, stirring constantly until all is absorbed
(Add water if more liquid is needed)
When rice is cooked, remove from heat and let cool for at least 10 minutes
Stir in parmesan and eggs
Season with black pepper
Spoon into a lightly greased 22 cm springform pan
Bake in preheated oven until set, about 30 minutes
Allow to rest for a few minutes
Cut into slices and serve with a few drops of olive oil

• Cake can be made a day in advance. Cut into slices and reheat just before serving

# Baked Salmon with Small Beets

## Serves 2

6 small beetroots
1 tsp vegetable oil
1 tbsp lemon juice
1 tsp sea salt
½ tsp freshly ground black pepper
400 g Norwegian salmon
100 ml Mint Crème Fraîche

Set oven to 180 °C
Wrap beetroots in foil and bake in preheated oven until soft, about 45 minutes
Let cool and remove skins
Cut into wedges, cover and set aside
Set oven to 190 °C
Mix oil, lemon juice, salt and pepper together and rub into salmon
Place on a baking tray and bake in preheated oven for 10 minutes
Serve with beetroot wedges and Mint Crème Fraîche

## Mint Crème Fraîche

100 ml crème fraîche
1 tsp finely chopped fresh mint leaves
1 tsp finely chopped fresh dill

Mix ingredients together

# White Choc Cookies with Rose Cloud

100 g unsalted butter, softened
100 g sugar
1 egg
1 tsp vanilla extract or paste
1 cup self-raising flour
½ cup oats
½ cup desiccated coconut
½ cup mixed nuts, chopped
200 g white chocolate, chopped

Set oven to 180 °C
Cream butter and sugar in a mixing bowl
Add egg and vanilla, and mix well
Sift in flour and fold through
Stir in oats, coconut, nuts and chocolate
Spoon small amounts of mixture onto two baking trays
Bake in preheated oven for 10 to 12 minutes
(Remove before edges brown too much)
Let rest for 1 minute
Carefully lift onto wire racks
Serve with Rose Cloud

## Rose Cloud

250 g soft mascarpone
1 heaped tbsp icing sugar
2 tbsp white muscadel
1 tsp rose water

Remove the mascarpone from the refrigerator 1 hour in advance
Spoon into a mixing bowl
Stir in the rest of the ingredients
Serve at room temperature

# Rehearsal Food

Nobody on earth is more kind-hearted, dedicated and determined than a well-fed musician. For years I've been wondering if the success of our stage shows is the result of our skills and hard work or simply because we eat so well!

Rehearsals always take place at my house; there is enough space AND A KITCHEN! A typical rehearsal day consists of two three-hour sessions. Everybody arrives at 09h00, and I serve coffee, muffins and fruit. Then comes the first session, followed by lunch. The menu always includes dishes such as breads and cakes that can be prepared a day ahead. The rest of the food comes from the oven and takes only a few minutes to prepare, garnish and plate.

Every night I stand on stage with some of this country's most talented musicians. They are not only my friends and colleagues, they are also my support structure and inspiration. Cheers to all of you!

MENU

Asparagus and Feta Salad

Nut and Seed Loaf

Roast Chicken with Buttered Mushrooms

Upside-Down Mango Cake

# Asparagus and Feta Salad

500 g fresh asparagus
1 tbsp vegetable oil
sea salt
freshly ground black pepper
Mustard Dressing
100 g feta
2 tbsp almond flakes, lightly roasted

Set oven to 180 °C
Toss asparagus with oil
Arrange on an oven tray and roast in preheated oven until
cooked but still firm, about 7 or 8 minutes
Season with salt and pepper and let cool
Arrange on a serving dish
Drizzle with Mustard Dressing
Sprinkle with feta and almonds

## Mustard Dressing

¼ cup extra virgin olive oil
juice of 1 lemon
1 tbsp honey
1 tsp Dijon mustard
pinch of salt
½ tsp freshly ground black pepper

Mix ingredients together until smooth

# Nut and Seed Loaf

2 cups brown-bread flour
1 cup Nutty Wheat
2 tsp bicarbonate of soda
1 tsp salt
1½ cups mixed nuts, chopped
2 tbsp sunflower seeds
2 tbsp pumpkin seeds
2 tsp sesame seeds
2 tsp poppy seeds
½ cup vegetable oil
2 eggs, beaten
2 tbsp honey

Set oven to 170 °C
Combine ingredients in a large mixing bowl
Using hands, work into a sticky dough
Divide between two medium-sized bread pans, lightly greased
Bake in preheated oven for 1 hour

# Roast Chicken with Buttered Mushrooms

2 medium chickens
20 cloves garlic, unpeeled
1 cup dry white wine
1 cup chicken stock
sea salt
freshly ground black pepper
200 g baby carrots
600 g fresh mushrooms, 3 or 4 different varieties
2 tbsp butter
handful of fresh flat-leaf parsley

Set oven to 170 °C
Place chickens in a large oven dish
Add garlic, wine and stock
Season with salt and pepper
Cover and bake in preheated oven for 45 minutes
Add carrots, cover and bake for 15 more minutes
Remove from oven and baste with sauce in the dish
Return to oven and roast, uncovered, for 20 more minutes
While chickens are roasting, clean mushrooms and slice into large strips
Melt butter in a saucepan
Add mushrooms and let simmer over low heat for 20 minutes
Take dish out of the oven and place chickens on a large serving dish
Add carrots to mushrooms and stir
Taste and add salt, if needed
Spoon around chickens
Drizzle with sauce from oven dish
Garnish with parsley and serve

# Upside-Down Mango Cake

## Sauce

80 g butter
¼ cup brown sugar

Heat butter and sugar in a small saucepan and
stir constantly until sugar has dissolved

## Cake

2 ripe mangoes, peeled and sliced
1 cup butter, softened at room temperature
1½ cups brown sugar
2 eggs, beaten
1¼ cups self-raising flour
¼ cup milk
1 cup pecan nuts, chopped
1 tsp mixed spice
½ tsp ground cinnamon

Set oven to 170 °C
Wrap outside (bottom and sides) of a 22 cm springform pan with tinfoil
Spread sauce over base of pan
Arrange mango slices on top
Cream butter and sugar in a mixing bowl
Beat in eggs
Sift in flour and mix
Mix in milk
Add nuts, spice and cinnamon, and mix
Spoon over mango slices
Bake in preheated oven for 50 minutes
Let cool and run a thin-bladed knife around sides of pan to loosen cake
Turn out onto a serving plate

# Easter Sunday

Apart from commercial hot cross buns and Easter eggs, South Africans don't seem to have any traditional Easter fare. As schools close during this time, most people do a quick getaway and churchgoers attend special services, but few people seem to go to the trouble of preparing cakes, breads, pastries, dishes or table settings as they do for Christmas.

Mourning the death of Christ and celebrating His resurrection should be the perfect time to reminisce, reflect and get together with family, friends and fellow worshippers. Some of the world's most beautiful music has been composed for this time, and nature offers all the beauty and riches of autumn. There is no better time to create and enjoy an unforgettable meal.

MENU

Potato and Cauliflower Soup

Steak Pies

Roasted Pumpkin

Tapioca Fig Pudding

# Potato and Cauliflower Soup

500 g potatoes, peeled and cut into cubes
500 g cauliflower, broken into florets
2 cups chicken or vegetable stock
2 cups water
grated zest of 1 lemon
sea salt
freshly ground black pepper
5 parsnips, peeled and cut into strips
1 tbsp vegetable oil
1 tbsp crème fraîche
handful of finely chopped fresh parsley

Set oven to 180 °C
Place the first five ingredients in a saucepan
Season with salt and pepper
Bring to the boil and let simmer for 30 minutes
Toss parsnips with oil and bake in preheated oven until starting to brown,
about 25 minutes
Remove soup from heat and purée
Stir in crème fraîche
Spoon into bowls
Arrange parsnip strips on top, sprinkle with parsley and serve

# Steak Pies

### Serves 8

3 tbsp butter
1 large onion, chopped
4 tbsp flour
1 tsp sea salt
1 tsp freshly ground black pepper
1 kg rump steak, cut into 1,5 cm x 1,5 cm cubes
2 tbsp vegetable or grapeseed oil
2 tbsp brandy
1 tbsp soy sauce
6 tbsp water
leaves of 6 sprigs of thyme
2 eggs
pinch of salt

Set oven to 180 °C
Heat 1 tbsp butter in a saucepan
Add onion and caramelise over low heat, about 1 hour, set aside
In a mixing bowl, combine 2 tbsp flour with salt and pepper
Add meat cubes and toss until covered
Heat oil in a frying pan and brown meat for 5 minutes
Add brandy, soy sauce, water and thyme
Lower heat, cover and let simmer for 25 minutes
(Add a little more water if needed)
When meat is soft and sauce has thickened, spoon into eight ramekins
Melt 2 tbsp butter, add to 2 tbsp flour in a mixing bowl
Mix to a paste
Add eggs and mix well
Season with salt and spoon over meat
Bake in preheated oven for 30 minutes

# Roasted Pumpkin

1 medium pumpkin
2 tbsp vegetable or grapeseed oil
juice of 1 lemon
sea salt
freshly ground black pepper
2 tbsp Tomato Chilli Jam (recipe on page 187)
2 tbsp pumpkin seeds, roasted

Set oven to 180 °C
Cut pumpkin into slices and remove seeds
Mix oil and lemon juice, and brush over pumpkin
Arrange on a baking tray and roast in preheated oven until cooked and
edges start to blacken, about 45 minutes
Remove from oven, and season with salt and pepper
Spoon Tomato Chilli Jam over each slice
Return to oven and bake for 5 more minutes
Remove from oven and sprinkle with pumpkin seeds

# Tapioca Fig Pudding

1 cup tapioca
1 ℓ milk
⅓ cup sugar
2 eggs, beaten
1 tsp vanilla extract
16 fresh figs
1 tbsp honey
1 tbsp butter

Cover tapioca with water and soak for 3 hours
Drain off excess water
Set oven to 180 °C
Heat tapioca, milk and sugar in a saucepan
Stir over medium heat until the tapioca is cooked
Remove from heat and let cool for 10 minutes
Stir in eggs and vanilla
Spoon into an oven dish
Cut a cross in the top of each fig and arrange on top of the tapioca
Heat honey and butter together, and drizzle over figs
Bake in preheated oven for 35 minutes

# Midweek Abundance

My grandparents lived in Wellington in a tiny little house, a magical place filled with laughter, surprises and the smell of home cooking. My most vivid memory of that house is that the front door was always open, especially during mealtimes. Summer or winter, there were always people going in and out, staying for a few minutes or a whole evening, having a quick bite or sitting down to a feast. My grandmother had no idea what a glamorous and tireless hostess she was.

Nowadays we have much busier lives, gruelling schedules and enormous workloads. I regularly find myself trying to change the pattern or to escape from any possible routine. I find few things as rejuvenating and energising as entertaining friends in the middle of the week.

A few candles, some pretty flowers, a bottle of wine and a simple but hearty meal, and you have a celebration. The next day you might feel a little tired, even somewhat fragile, but the pleasure absolutely justifies the suffering.

MENU

Berry Cocktail

Rolled Pizza

Lemon and Orange Chicken

Ginger Date Puddings

# Berry Cocktail

## per serving

crushed ice
60 ml Irish whiskey
100 ml cranberry juice
40 ml puréed mixed berries
60 ml Lemon Syrup
3 ice cubes

Fill a tall glass two-thirds with crushed ice
Combine next four ingredients in a cocktail shaker
Add 3 ice cubes and shake
Pour over crushed ice, and serve

## Lemon Syrup

1 cup sugar
juice of 3 lemons
¾ cup water

Heat ingredients in a saucepan
Stir until sugar has dissolved
Allow to boil for 1 minute
Remove from heat and let cool

# Rolled Pizza

2 tbsp tomato paste
2 store-bought pizza bases
1¼ cups grated mozzarella or cheddar
120 g green olives, stuffed with anchovies
freshly ground black pepper
extra virgin olive oil
fresh rocket leaves

Set oven to 180 °C
Spread tomato paste over pizza bases
Sprinkle cheese over
Cut olives in half and arrange on top
Season with black pepper
Bake in preheated oven for 5 minutes
Remove from oven and roll up pizzas
Secure with toothpicks
Return to oven and bake for 5 more minutes
Remove from oven and cut into slices
Arrange on a serving platter, and drizzle lightly with olive oil
Top with rocket leaves, and serve

# Lemon and Orange Chicken

12 chicken thighs
½ cup chicken stock
juice of 1 lemon
juice of 1 orange
grated zest of ½ lemon
grated zest of ½ orange
12 soft dried apricots
4 red or orange bell peppers, seeded and quartered
sea salt
freshly ground black pepper
¼ cup finely chopped fresh parsley
½ cup finely chopped fresh mint

Set oven to 180 °C
Place first eight ingredients in an oven dish
Season with salt and pepper
Cover and bake in preheated oven for 1 hour
Remove from oven and baste with sauce in the dish
Return to oven and bake uncovered for 10 more minutes
Remove from oven, cover and let rest for 5 minutes
Transfer to a serving platter and sprinkle with chopped herbs

# Ginger Date Puddings

250 g dates, pitted and chopped
½ cup boiling water
½ cup Irish whiskey
½ cup soft butter
¾ cup demerara sugar
2 eggs, lightly beaten
1½ cups self-raising flour
pinch of salt
75 g glazed cherries, chopped
3 tsp chopped fresh ginger
100 g preserved figs, chopped
6 or 8 tsp whiskey, extra
200 ml fresh cream

Set oven to 180 °C
Combine dates and water in a mixing bowl
Add whiskey and let cool
In a separate bowl, beat butter and sugar until creamy
Beat in eggs
Sift in flour, add salt and mix well
Mix in cherries, ginger and figs
Spoon into six ovenproof cups or small bowls
(Use eight cups or bowls if smaller portions are preferred)
Place in a baking pan filled with water up to about a third the height of the cups
Bake in preheated oven for 30 minutes
Remove from oven and pour 1 tsp whiskey over each pudding
Serve with cream

# George Turns Nine

George is one of my godchildren and definitely one of my most favourite people on this planet. Unique, temperamental and totally unpredictable, he has changed my life in many ways. He is confident, energetic, super-intelligent and very talented, but (I suspect) totally bored with school activities and ordinary life. I have spent many, many hours over the past nine years trying to come up with ideas, games, stories and books that will fascinate him.

Since George's birth I have been involved in the preparations for every one of his birthdays. We have constructed gingerbread castles, baked trucks, trains and superheroes, and decorated rooms in every possible theme. For his ninth birthday I decided on a galactic theme with stars, planets and spaceships in black, white and silver. Everything had to be fantastical and fun, but masculine and mature. The menu had to reflect his favourite foods, prepared in a delicious but healthy way.

MENU

Alien Juice

Oven Chips with Yogurt Dip

Birthday Burgers

Chocolate Star Cakes

Blueberry Jelly with Thick Custard

# Alien Juice

## per serving

125 ml clear apple juice
125 ml white grape juice
handful of black grapes, frozen

Pour juices into a tall glass and add grapes

# Oven Chips with Yogurt Dip

2 kg potatoes
2 tbsp vegetable oil
sea salt

Set oven to 180 °C
Peel potatoes and cut into thin slices
Toss with oil and arrange on a baking tray
Bake in preheated oven for 45 to 55 minutes
Remove from oven and season lightly with salt
Serve with Yogurt Dip

## Yogurt Dip

2 tbsp tomato purée
2 tbsp brown sugar
2 tbsp balsamic vinegar
2 tbsp water
1½ cups plain yogurt

Heat first four ingredients in a saucepan
Stir until sugar has dissolved
Remove from heat and let cool
Stir into yogurt

# Birthday Burgers

1 tbsp butter
2 medium onions, chopped
sea salt
250 g lean bacon
6 panini, 6 cm x 15 cm each
120 g cheddar, grated

Heat butter in a saucepan
Add onions and caramelise over low heat, about 1 hour
Remove from heat and season lightly with salt
Place bacon in a cool pan
Fry over medium heat until golden brown on each side
Slice panini in half horizontally
Spread onions over bottom half
Top with bacon strips and grated cheese
Cover with other panini halves
Grill on both sides in a hot griddle pan until cheese has melted
Cut into smaller portions and serve

# Chocolate Star Cakes

1 cup unsalted butter, softened at room temperature
1 cup castor sugar
1 tsp vanilla extract
4 eggs
1 cup self-raising flour
3 tbsp cocoa powder
¼ cup milk

Set oven to 180 °C
Beat butter, sugar and vanilla with an electric mixer until soft and creamy
Add eggs one at a time, beating well after each addition
Add flour and cocoa, and beat well
Beat in milk
Spoon batter evenly into 15 lightly greased muffin-pan cups
Bake in preheated oven for 15 minutes
Remove muffins from pan and cool on a wire rack
Decorate with Snow Icing and silver balls

## Snow Icing

2½ cups icing sugar
5 tbsp boiling water

Sift icing sugar into a mixing bowl
Add water and mix until smooth

# Blueberry Jelly with Thick Custard

900 ml blueberry juice
2 drops blue food colouring
7 tbsp water
7 tbsp gelatine

Taste juice and sweeten if necessary
Stir in food colouring
Pour water into a small saucepan
Sprinkle gelatine over
Heat slowly until gelatine has dissolved
Stir into juice
Pour into glasses, filling them to about two-thirds
Refrigerate until set
Top with Thick Custard, cover and refrigerate until serving

## Thick Custard

2 cups milk
1 tsp vanilla extract
½ cup sugar
6 egg yolks
2 tsp cornflour

Combine milk, vanilla and sugar in a saucepan
Stir over medium heat until sugar has dissolved
Remove from heat and let cool for a few minutes
Beat egg yolks in a mixing bowl
In a separate small bowl, stir 1 or 2 tbsp milk into cornflour, and mix to a paste
Beat paste into eggs
Beat 2 tbsp of the warm milk into egg mixture
Whisk egg mixture into milk
Stir with whisk over low heat until custard has thickened
Remove from heat, press through a sieve and let cool

# With Friends on a Cold, Cold Night

I know many people who enjoy sitting on chairs, armchairs, giant comfortable chairs, sofas and couches. Some put their feet up, others casually lean over to one side, holding a glass. May they find happiness. I prefer sitting at a table, holding a fork. And I LOVE people who enjoy doing this with me.

A great number of my friends spend as much time at the table as I do. We sit for hours, waiting for the meal, enjoying the meal, talking about the meal, drinking bottles and bottles of good wine, playing games (yes, we do!), looking at books or pictures, laughing and, most importantly, planning the next meal.

The pleasure of an evening like this doubles in winter with the added joy of a fireplace and hundreds of candles, always festive (and kind to the complexion), no matter how late it gets.

At my house, meals like these almost always include pies and cakes, foods that can be prepared well in advance and do not keep me away from the company.

MENU

Ciabatta and Baby Spinach

Potato Wedge Salad

Mushroom Pie and Green Beans with Ginger and Sesame Seeds

Strawberry Cherry Cake

# Ciabatta and Baby Spinach

1 tbsp vegetable oil
2 cloves garlic, finely chopped
grated zest of ½ lemon
200 g baby spinach leaves
130 g feta
sea salt
freshly ground black pepper
6 ciabatta rolls
2 tbsp olive oil

Heat vegetable oil, garlic and zest in a pan
Add spinach and stir until spinach has wilted
Remove from heat and stir in feta
Season with salt and pepper
Cut rolls in half and brush insides with olive oil
Spoon spinach mixture onto bottom half of each roll
Cover with top half and cut into slices

# Potato Wedge Salad

6 large potatoes

2 tbsp vegetable oil

sea salt

300 g *petits pois*

handful of fresh watercress

100 g parmesan, shaved

freshly ground black pepper


Set oven to 180 °C

Wash potatoes, dry and cut into wedges

Toss with oil and arrange on a baking sheet

Bake in preheated oven until golden brown

Season with salt and let cool

Arrange on individual plates

Spoon *petits pois* over

Arrange watercress and parmesan shavings on top

Drizzle with Sour Cream Dressing, season with black pepper, and serve


## Sour Cream Dressing

8 tbsp extra virgin olive oil

3 tbsp sour cream

juice of 1 lemon

2 tbsp brown sugar

1 clove garlic, crushed

sea salt

freshly ground black pepper


Whisk ingredients together

Cover and refrigerate

Remove from refrigerator 30 minutes before serving

# Mushroom Pie and Green Beans with Ginger and Sesame Seeds

1 tbsp butter
2 cloves garlic, finely chopped
1 small red chilli, seeded and finely chopped
400 g white button mushrooms
400 g large brown mushrooms
200 g shiitake mushrooms
200 g porcini mushrooms
100 g fettuccine, uncooked
3 tbsp finely grated parmesan
1 tbsp heavy cream
1 tbsp strong chutney
2 heaped tbsp finely chopped parsley
sea salt
freshly ground black pepper
2 sheets frozen puff pastry, thawed

Set oven to 180 °C
Heat butter, garlic and chilli in a
large pan
Add all the mushrooms and simmer
over low heat until soft
Break fettuccine and cook in lightly
salted water until al dente
Drain pasta and stir into mushrooms
Add parmesan, cream, chutney and
parsley
Season with salt and pepper
Roll out pastry until almost doubled
in size
Line bottom and sides of a large square
or rectangular pie dish with pastry

Spoon in mushroom filling and
top with the rest of pastry
Seal joins carefully and prick top
once or twice with a fork
Bake in preheated oven until pastry
is cooked, about 40 minutes
Serve with Green Beans with
Ginger and Sesame Seeds

## Green Beans with Ginger and Sesame Seeds

1 tbsp vegetable oil
1 tbsp crushed ginger
1 tbsp honey
juice of ½ lemon
200 g slender green beans
1 tsp sesame seeds
sea salt

Heat oil, ginger, honey and
lemon juice in a saucepan
Stir in beans and let simmer
for 5 minutes
Stir in seeds and remove from heat
Season lightly with salt

# Strawberry Cherry Cake

150 g butter, softened at room temperature
1 cup sugar
1 tsp vanilla extract
4 eggs
1¼ cups self-raising flour, sifted
1 tbsp poppy seeds
8 fresh strawberries, quartered
16 maraschino cherries, halved
champagne

Set oven to 180 °C
Line the bottom of a 22 cm springform pan with baking paper
Grease lightly and dust with flour
Cream together butter, sugar and vanilla in a mixing bowl
In a separate bowl, whisk eggs until light and fluffy
Mix into butter and sugar mixture
Add flour and poppy seeds, and fold in with a metal spoon
Mix in strawberries and cherries
Spoon batter into springform pan and bake in preheated oven for 50 minutes
(If cake browns too quickly, cover loosely with foil)
Let cool for 10 minutes, then remove from the pan
Cut into slices and serve drizzled with champagne

• As the berry pieces are chunky, they may sink to the bottom of the cake
Still, I prefer biting into slightly bigger pieces of fruit

# Workday Fuel

A normal day at my house is one filled with people. We work, have meetings, plan events, fit costumes, take pictures, design new products AND EAT. No matter how close the deadline, hectic the schedule or great the stress, we have the most wonderful lunches.

We take turns in cooking, each of us has his or her specialities. The food is simple, tasty, substantial, hearty and healthy; it gives us energy and makes us happy. Certain dishes are nearly always on the menu: wild or brown rice, good salads and sweet things that can serve both as a dessert and as a snack with tea. These are absolute favourites:

Olive Salad

Wild Rice and Lentils

Lamb Chops with Herbs

Sultana Tea Bread

# Olive Salad

1 cup boiling water
1 red onion, thinly sliced
100 g cos lettuce
3 hard-boiled eggs, quartered
1 cup black olives, pitted
1 cup green olives, pitted

In a small bowl, pour boiling water over onion slices
Let cool, and drain
Place cos leaves on a large serving platter
Arrange eggs, olives and onion on top
Serve with Pesto Dressing

## Pesto Dressing

2 tbsp Coriander and Cashew Pesto (recipe on page 188)
¼ cup extra virgin olive oil
2 tbsp white wine vinegar
1 tbsp honey
½ tsp freshly ground black pepper

Whisk ingredients together until smooth

• Pesto can be replaced by 2 tbsp finely chopped basil

# Wild Rice and Lentils

1 cup wild rice
½ cup brown rice
½ cup brown lentils, rinsed
½ tsp curry powder
1 tbsp soy sauce
1 tbsp balsamic vinegar
2 cups chicken or vegetable stock
6 cups water
1 large onion, chopped
1 green bell pepper, seeded and chopped
1 tomato, chopped
1 tbsp olive oil
2 tbsp finely chopped fresh parsley

Combine first eight ingredients in a saucepan
Bring to the boil and cook over medium heat for 30 minutes
Add onion and bell pepper, continue cooking
(If more liquid is needed, add water a little at a time)
Remove from heat when rice is cooked
Stir in rest of ingredients

# Lamb Chops with Herbs

1 tbsp finely chopped fresh rosemary
1 tbsp finely chopped fresh parsley
1 tbsp finely chopped fresh thyme
2 cloves garlic, finely chopped
3 tbsp olive oil
juice and finely grated zest of 1 lemon
1 tbsp coarse sea salt
1 tbsp freshly ground black pepper
12 lamb chops, French cut

Mix first eight ingredients to a paste
Rub into chops
Cover and leave in a cool place for 3 hours
Cook in a very hot griddle pan for 3 minutes per side

# Sultana Tea Bread

2¼ cups self-raising flour
1 cup strong black tea (Ceylon, Rooibos or Earl Grey)
2 eggs, beaten
1 cup sugar
1 cup golden sultanas
½ cup raisins

Sift flour into a mixing bowl
Add tea and mix well
Mix in eggs and sugar
Mix in sultanas and raisins
Cover and let rest for 1 hour
In the meantime, preheat the oven to 170 °C
Pour batter into a lightly greased loaf pan and bake for 45 minutes

# Hocus Pocus

My favourite movie of all time is *Hocus Pocus*, a ridiculous tale of three witches who will stop at nothing in their quest for eternal life. A typical Walt Disney production, it consists of 92 minutes of chaos, magic, fantasy and comedy until finally good triumphs over evil. Bette Midler's performance as the oldest witch is the funniest, most over-the-top, most brilliant thing I have ever seen. And I have seen it a million times, I know every word, every hand movement, every roll of the eyes.

There has never been a visitor to my house who hasn't been forced to watch it, sometimes the whole thing, sometimes highlights with narration. Finally it had to happen: An official Hocus Pocus Night for all those who join me in my devotion to this unprecedented piece of entertainment, also for those who still need to be educated. And, of course, a menu was devised to go with it:

Popcorn for the Brave

Butternut and Mozzarella Open Pie

Anxiety Cake

Witches' Brew

# Popcorn for the Brave

2 tbsp butter
½ tsp cayenne pepper
8 drops Tabasco
½ tsp paprika
200 g popcorn, uncooked

In a small saucepan, heat butter with pepper, Tabasco and paprika
Pop the corn in a large pot or microwave
Pour spicy butter over and stir to coat

# Butternut and Mozzarella Open Pie

500 g butternut, peeled and cut into 2,5 cm x 2,5 cm cubes
1 tbsp vegetable oil
1 sheet frozen puff pastry, thawed
200 g mozzarella, cut into 1,5 cm x 1,5 cm cubes
200 g cocktail tomatoes, pierced
sea salt
freshly ground black pepper
handful of fresh rocket

Set oven to 180 °C
Toss butternut with oil and arrange on a baking tray
Bake in preheated oven for 20 minutes, let cool and turn out onto a plate
Place puff pastry on baking tray and press down gently
Prick bottom with a fork and mark edges with a knife
Arrange butternut, mozzarella and tomatoes in rows on top of pastry
Return to oven and bake until pastry is golden brown, about 25 minutes
Remove from oven and season with salt and pepper
Garnish with rocket just before serving
Serve hot or cold

# Anxiety Cake

1½ cups butter
2 cups castor sugar
6 eggs, beaten
1½ cups self-raising flour
1½ cups ground almonds
juice and finely grated zest of 1½ oranges
1 drop yellow food colouring
1 drop red food colouring

Set oven to 170 °C
Cream butter and sugar in a mixing bowl
Add eggs and mix well
Stir in flour and almonds
Add juice, zest and food colourings, and mix well
Divide batter between two lightly greased 22 cm springform pans
Bake in preheated oven for 35 minutes
Remove from pans and let cool
Use Black Icing to sandwich cakes together and spread over the top

## Black Icing

200 g icing sugar
100 g butter, softened at room temperature
1 tbsp Van Der Hum liqueur
few drops of black food colouring

Mix ingredients together until creamy

# Witches' Brew

250 ml fresh cream
1 tbsp castor sugar
100 g dark chocolate
6 tbsp whisky
1,2 ℓ freshly brewed black coffee

Beat cream and sugar until soft peaks form
Shave a few curls off chocolate and reserve for decoration
Break rest of chocolate into pieces and divide among six glasses
Pour 1 tbsp whisky over chocolate in each glass
Fill rest of glass with coffee
Spoon cream on top and sprinkle with chocolate shavings
Serve immediately

# Stork Tea with Men

Wess-Lee not only manages my office, but she is also a great singer who has performed in many of my stage productions. When she was expecting her second child, I decided to surprise her with a morning tea. I also decided to invite singers and musicians who have worked with her. It turned out to be a men only party!

The food was pretty, decadent and delicious. I prepared two of my favourite treats: The Flaky Chocolate Cake is a rustic concoction which bakes into a mousse surrounded by a flaky crust, while The Only Cheesecake is the result of many efforts to create a cheesecake not as dense, dull and dry as the typical baked version, nor as cheap-looking and -tasting as the standard unbaked variety. The final result: Heaven! The first, last and only cheesecake I'll ever make.

MENU

Sparkling Ice Tea

Smoked Salmon Tartlets

Vanilla Yogurt Cakes with Rose Frosting

Flaky Chocolate Cake

The Only Cheesecake

# Sparkling Ice Tea

## per serving

orange wedges
chilled Ceylon tea, sweetened with honey
champagne or Cap Classique

Place 2 or 3 orange wedges in a champagne flute
Fill glass halfway with tea
Top with champagne

• The mother-to-be is served ice tea with no champagne

# Smoked Salmon Tartlets

1 sheet frozen shortcrust pastry, thawed
1 tbsp finely grated parmesan
1 tbsp freshly ground black pepper
250 ml fresh cream
pinch of salt
1 tbsp finely chopped fresh parsley
1 tbsp finely chopped fresh chives
150 g smoked salmon, cut into narrow strips
extra fresh chives, cut into 3 cm lengths for garnishing

Set oven to 180 °C
Place pastry on a floured surface
Sprinkle one half with parmesan and pepper, then fold empty half over
Roll out thinly, cut into circles and line 24 small muffin-pan cups
Prick with fork and bake in preheated oven until golden
Let cool and store in an airtight container
Whip cream until soft peaks form
Stir in salt and chopped herbs
Spoon filling into pastry cases
Place strips of salmon on top and garnish with chives

# Vanilla Yogurt Cakes with Rose Frosting

1 cup self-raising flour

1 cup ground almonds

1 cup sugar

pinch of salt

2 eggs, beaten

1¼ cups plain yogurt

seeds from 1 vanilla pod

Set oven to 180 °C

Sift flour into a mixing bowl

Stir in almonds, sugar and salt

In a separate bowl, beat together eggs, yogurt and vanilla seeds

Stir into flour mixture

Fill 12 large muffin-pan cups to about two-thirds and bake in preheated oven for

15 minutes

Let cool and top with Rose Frosting

## Rose Frosting

1½ cups icing sugar

5 tbsp boiling water

1 tsp rose water

1 drop red food colouring

1 drop yellow food colouring

Mix ingredients together until smooth

# Flaky Chocolate Cake

200 g butter
200 g dark chocolate
5 eggs, separated
1¼ cups castor sugar
¼ cup plain flour
1 cup ground almonds
1 tsp vanilla extract
1 tbsp balsamic vinegar

Set oven to 170 °C
Grease and line a 22 cm springform pan
Wrap outside (bottom and sides) with tin foil to prevent leaking
Melt butter and chocolate over low heat, let cool for a few minutes
In a mixing bowl, beat egg yolks and castor sugar until creamy
Beat in melted chocolate
Stir in flour and almonds
Stir in vanilla and vinegar
In a separate bowl, beat egg whites until stiff peaks form
Fold into chocolate mixture
Pour into pan and bake in preheated oven for 1 hour
Let cool for 20 minutes and remove from pan

# The Only Cheesecake

75 g ginger biscuits, crushed
75 g pecan nuts, chopped
75 g butter, melted
4 eggs, separated
1¼ cups castor sugar
250 g cream cheese
250 ml crème fraîche
250 ml natural yogurt
pinch of nutmeg
1 tsp vanilla extract
¼ tsp ginger
½ tbsp ground cinnamon
pinch of salt

Set oven to 170 °C
Lightly grease and line the base of a 22 cm springform pan
Wrap outside (bottom and sides) with tinfoil to prevent leaking
Combine biscuits, nuts and butter, mix well and press over bottom of pan
In a mixing bowl, beat egg yolks and castor sugar until creamy
Add remaining ingredients except egg whites, and beat well
In a separate bowl, beat egg whites until stiff peaks form
Fold into cream cheese mixture
Pour into pan and bake in preheated oven for 1 hour
Let cool and remove from pan

# Princess's Picnic

Dali is George's younger sister, a beautiful, gentle, fairy-like little thing. When she came to this earth we all fell in love with her immediately. A well-known spiritual guide once contacted me out of the blue to tell me that there was a little girl in my life who was able to see things most of us couldn't, who could communicate with creatures from other worlds and who had very special powers. That girl is Dali.

Dali has always loved anything pink and girly and has always been treated like a princess, so when I started planning her sixth birthday party, there were only three words: pink, princess and picnic.

The food had to be beautiful and as natural as possible – half the world's children are hysterical because of the toxic things they are fed at parties. We also had to include some of the birthday girl's favourites, thus the meringues and the tiny meatballs.

MENU

Strawberry Milk

Chewy Meringues

Mini Meatballs

Small Cheese and Onion Pizzas

Butterfly Cakes

Cake for the Mothers

# Strawberry Milk

## per serving

200 ml low-fat milk
2 tbsp Strawberry Syrup

Whisk together until foamy
Pour into a tall glass or mug

## Strawberry Syrup

500 g fresh strawberries, chopped
¼ cup sugar
¼ cup water
1 tsp vanilla extract

Heat ingredients in a saucepan and let simmer for 10 minutes
Let cool and purée in a food processor
Cover and refrigerate

# Chewy Meringues

### Makes 24

3 egg whites
110 g castor sugar
¼ tsp cream of tartar
1 drop red natural food colouring
2 tbsp cornflour
1 tbsp icing sugar
100 g strawberry wafers, crushed

Set oven to 110 °C
Beat egg whites in a clean bowl with an electric mixer until foamy
Add cream of tartar and 1 tsp of the castor sugar, beat for 1 minute
Add remaining castor sugar 1 tsp at a time, beating for at least 30 seconds
between additions
Add colouring and beat for 6 more minutes until egg whites are very smooth and
stiff peaks form
Sift cornflour and icing sugar together and gently fold in
Fold in the crushed wafers
Line a baking sheet with wax paper
With a teaspoon, drop mounds of meringue onto it
Bake in preheated oven for 1 hour
Turn off heat and leave meringues in the oven while it cools down
When completely cool, store in an airtight container

# Mini Meatballs

## Makes about 80

500 g lean beef mince
500 g spicy sausage meat
1 egg
1 tbsp sweet chilli sauce
2 cloves garlic, finely chopped (optional)
pinch of nutmeg
2 heaped tbsp finely chopped fresh parsley
sea salt
freshly ground black pepper

Set oven to 180 °C
Combine first seven ingredients in a mixing bowl
Season generously with salt and pepper, and mix well
Roll into 3 cm balls
Arrange on an oven tray and bake in preheated oven for 20 minutes
Shake halfway through cooking time

# Small Cheese and Onion Pizzas

1 tbsp butter
1 onion, chopped
sea salt
1 sheet frozen puff pastry, thawed
2 tbsp finely chopped fresh parsley
1 cup cheddar, grated
8 cherry tomatoes, sliced
extra chopped parsley for garnishing

Set oven to 180 °C
Heat butter in a saucepan, add onion and caramelise over low heat, about 1 hour
Remove from heat and season lightly with salt
Roll out pastry and cut out eight circles of about 10 cm in diameter
Use a knife to mark the edges, and pierce the insides with a fork
Spread a small amount of onion over each
Sprinkle with cheese and arrange slices of tomato on top
Place on an oven tray and bake in preheated oven until golden, 20 to 25 minutes
Remove from oven and sprinkle with a little parsley

• For adults, freshly ground black pepper can be added to the mixture and more
parsley sprinkled on top

# Butterfly Cakes

1 cup butter, softened at room temperature
1 cup sugar
3 eggs
1 tsp vanilla extract
1 cup self-raising flour
¼ cup dried cranberries
1½ tbsp cocoa powder
butterfly sprinkles
paper or silk butterflies, mounted on toothpicks

Set oven to 170 °C
In a mixing bowl, cream together butter and sugar
Beat in eggs and vanilla
Sift in flour and mix
Stir in cranberries
Divide batter in half and mix cocoa into one half
Fill 12 small ring moulds a quarter each with chocolate mixture
Top with the same amount of vanilla mixture
Bake in preheated oven for 15 to 20 minutes
Turn out onto a wire rack and let cool
Fill holes with Soft Vanilla Icing
Decorate with butterfly sprinkles and paper or silk butterflies

## Soft Vanilla Icing

½ cup butter, softened at room temperature
2 cups icing sugar, sifted
1 tbsp warm water
1 tsp vanilla paste

Mix together until creamy

# Cake for the Mothers

½ cup butter
1 cup sugar
3 eggs
1 tsp vanilla extract
1 cup (250 ml) crème fraîche
1 cup self-raising flour, sifted
½ cup ground almonds
½ cup dessicated coconut
2 tbsp strawberry liqueur
Mascarpone Icing
small white and pink marshmallows

Set oven to 170 °C
Lightly grease and line the base of a 22 cm springform pan
Wrap outside (bottom and sides) with tinfoil to prevent leaking
Cream butter and sugar in a mixing bowl
Beat in eggs and vanilla
Mix in crème fraîche
Fold in sifted flour
Mix in almonds and coconut
Pour into springform pan
Bake in preheated oven for 50 minutes
Remove from oven and drizzle with liqueur
Let cool and decorate with Mascarpone Icing
Top with marshmallows

## Mascarpone Icing

250 g mascarpone
2 cups icing sugar, sifted
1 tbsp strawberry liqueur

Mix ingredients together until smooth

# Table for Two

I have been friends with Charlene for almost fifteen years. I met her when I had to perform at an event she had organised. The night before, a rainstorm nearly destroyed the marquee. I was on my way to complain about all the water in my dressing room, when she told somebody else to be quiet and sit down, so I did as well. When we met again, we discovered we had many things in common, and became great friends.

We both have strong opinions about many things, but we have very similar tastes in decoration. We both love shopping, have survived travelling together, are workaholics and collect extraordinary books. Charlene enjoys travelling and eating at restaurants much more than I do, but when we are together we prefer dining at each other's houses, always with exquisite table settings. Over the years certain foods have become key elements, and most menus are inspired by these: Caesar salad, roast chicken, anything with chilli, oven-roasted butternut or sweet potatoes, and desserts with chocolate.

These recipes, of course, serve two.

MENU

Crostini Salad

Chicken Breasts with Mushroom and Sage Filling

Sweet Potato Fudge

Bleeding Hearts

# Crostini Salad

6 thin slices of baguette or baguette-shaped bread
6 anchovy fillets, quartered
6 thin slices white gouda
freshly ground black pepper
handful of butter lettuce leaves, rinsed and dried
Yogurt Dressing

Set oven to 180 °C
Place bread slices on an oven tray
Arrange four pieces of anchovy on each slice
Top with gouda
Bake crostini in preheated oven until golden
Season with black pepper
Place two or three crostini on a plate and top with lettuce leaves
Serve with small cups of Yogurt Dressing

## Yogurt Dressing

1 cup plain yogurt
1 anchovy fillet, chopped
1 tbsp finely grated parmesan
1 clove garlic, finely chopped

Mix ingredients together until smooth
Cover and refrigerate

# Chicken Breasts with Mushroom and Sage Filling

1 tbsp butter

4 large brown mushrooms, chopped

1 tbsp finely grated parmesan

½ cup brown-bread crumbs

1 tbsp finely chopped fresh sage

1 egg, beaten

2 tbsp water

sea salt

freshly ground black pepper

4 chicken breasts, deboned and skinned

4 rashers of bacon

1 tbsp vegetable oil

Heat butter and mushrooms in a saucepan, let simmer until mushrooms are
cooked, and let cool

Stir in parmesan, bread crumbs, sage, egg and water

Season with salt and pepper

Slice each chicken breast horizontally, leaving one side attached, and open out

Place between two sheets of clingfilm and pound until flattened

Remove clingfilm and place a rasher of bacon on each chicken breast

Spread with mushroom mixture

Place on a piece of clingfilm, roll up tightly and tie knots at both ends

Refrigerate for at least 1 hour

Bring water to the boil in a large saucepan

Add chicken rolls and cook in clingfilm for 15 minutes

Remove from water and let rest

Just before serving, heat oil in a frying pan

Remove chicken from clingfilm and brown over high heat for 1 minute

Cut into slices and serve with Sweet Potato Fudge (recipe on page 145)

# Sweet Potato Fudge

400 g sweet potatoes, peeled and cubed
1 tbsp vegetable oil
1 tbsp honey
1 tsp mustard seeds
¼ tsp ground ginger
sea salt
freshly ground black pepper

Set oven to 180 °C
Toss sweet potatoes with oil
Bake in preheated oven for 30 minutes
Heat honey, mustard seeds and ginger over low heat
Remove sweet potatoes from oven, and toss with honey glaze
Return to oven and bake for 5 more minutes
Season lightly with salt and pepper

# Bleeding Hearts

½ cup butter
½ cup castor sugar
2 eggs, beaten
½ cup self-raising flour, sifted
100 g dark chocolate
½ tsp vanilla extract
1 small red chilli, seeded and finely chopped
icing sugar

Set oven to 180 °C
Cream butter and sugar in a mixing bowl
Beat in eggs
Mix in sifted flour
Melt chocolate over low heat, and stir in vanilla and chilli
Fold into batter
Pour into six small heart-shaped moulds
Bake in preheated oven until just set on top
Carefully remove from mould, dust with icing sugar and serve immediately

• Use only ½ chilli, if preferred

# Small Foods

Small foods are tiny little nibbles that are eaten by hand and last no longer than one or two bites. They appear on trays or large plates at cocktail functions, fashion shows, church meetings, fundraisers, weddings, christenings, board meetings, game nights or book-club gatherings. They vary from dainty and elegant to experimental and tasteless, traditional and fattening, or greasy and tired.

I have been responsible for many opening nights at the theatre, book or CD launches and shop openings, but on these occasions the small foods have always been the responsibility of the caterers. I do not think I have ever invited anybody to my house for drinks or snacks – that does not make any sense – people come for a meal. I prepare small foods for when my guests arrive, just enough to soothe the wolf that awakes after a long day's work or give strength to those who will otherwise tell you the whole truth after only two sips of champagne.

These I serve often:

Geisha Potatoes

Cheese Frittatas

Pressed Panini

Smoked Trout Sandwiches

# Geisha Potatoes

500 g baby potatoes with skins, scrubbed
1 tbsp finely chopped fresh parsley
1 tbsp finely chopped fresh dill
½ tsp freshly ground black pepper
250 g cream or cottage cheese, softened at room temperature
fresh chives, tied in knots

Cook potatoes and let cool
Stir parsley, dill and pepper into cheese
Halve the potatoes and cut a sliver off the bottoms so they stand upright
Spread cheese mixture over top of each potato
Garnish with knotted chives, and season with a little ground black pepper

• Variation: Spoon a little caviar into the chive knots

# Cheese Frittatas

100 g soft goat's cheese
100 g mature cheddar, grated
½ cup finely chopped spring onions
2 tbsp plain flour
2 egg yolks
2 eggs, beaten
sea salt
freshly ground black pepper

Set oven to 170 °C
Crumble goat's cheese and portion evenly into twelve small non-stick
muffin-pan cups
Top with cheddar and spring onions
In a mixing bowl, blend flour and egg yolks to a paste
Add eggs and mix until creamy
Season with salt and pepper
Pour into muffin cups and bake in preheated oven until golden, about 20 minutes
Serve warm or at room temperature

# Pressed Panini

6 panini, about 6 cm x 15 cm
2 tbsp pesto
2 tbsp olive oil
2 red bell peppers, seeded, roasted and skinned
sea salt
250 g mozzarella in water, sliced thinly
freshly ground black pepper
handful of fresh basil
1 cup black olives, pitted and halved

Cut panini horizontally in half, and scoop out some of the soft part
Mix pesto and olive oil and brush on insides of panini
Cut peppers into strips and arrange on bottom half of each panini
Season lightly with salt
Top with mozzarella and season with pepper
Arrange basil and olives over the mozzarella
Cover with top halves of panini
Wrap tightly in wax paper
Group together and weigh down with a brick or
other heavy object placed on a tray
Let stand for 1 to 2 hours
Cut into slices

# Smoked Trout Sandwiches

250 g plain cream cheese, softened at room temperature
1 heaped tbsp finely chopped basil
1 heaped tbsp finely chopped chives
pinch of salt
½ tsp freshly ground black pepper
12 slices white bread
1 English cucumber, peeled, seeded and very thinly sliced
150 g smoked trout

Spoon cream cheese into a mixing bowl
Stir in basil, chives, salt and pepper
Spread lightly on all twelve slices of bread
Arrange cucumber on six of the slices
Top cucumber with strips of trout
Cover with remaining slices of bread
Remove crusts and cut into fingers

# Christmas Eve

My best childhood memories are those of Christmas celebrations at my grandmother's house. The entire family would get together in Wellington, and there were many of us! There was always a huge tree with tin angels and tiny candles, an overwhelming amount of food and a concert in the sitting room. That is where everything started for me, my love of special occasions, my weight problems and my need to be on stage.

Christmas is still the highlight of my year. I get as excited as any child. I start planning menus and decorations months ahead, and the first gifts are bought in August. There are several celebrations: one with godchildren, one with friends and, of course, one with family. Each event has its own theme, colours, table setting and menu. Menus differ, some are light and some are formal or traditional, some are without meat and some consist of guests' favourites – no matter how primitive some palates might be, happiness is what matters.

This is the one time of the year when I certainly do not believe in fast and easy food. The most important birthday of the year deserves some extra work. All things beautiful – lights, music, gifts, cakes, desserts and love – should be there.

## MENU

Giant Ginger Glass

Wise Men's Crowns

Leg of Lamb with Pea and Pepper Puffs

Picasso Trifle

# Giant Ginger Glass

Pulp 2 fresh pineapples in a food processor

## per serving

7 ice cubes
75 ml pineapple pulp
150 ml ginger beer
1 tbsp brandy
100 ml soda water

Place ice cubes in an oversized wine glass
Pour pineapple pulp over
Add rest of ingredients and serve immediately

# Wise Men's Crowns

1 cup brown rice
¾ cup wild rice
2 cups water
2 cups red wine
2 cups chicken stock
1 tbsp brown sugar
1 tbsp tomato paste
1 tomato, finely chopped
1 onion, finely chopped
2 cloves garlic, finely chopped
pinch of salt
pinch of black pepper
pinch of ground cinnamon
2 tbsp Greek yogurt

Combine all ingredients except yogurt
in a saucepan
Bring to the boil and cook over
medium heat until al dente, stirring
occasionally
Remove from heat and stir in yogurt
Taste and adjust seasoning, if necessary
Let cool to room temperature

## Confetti Salad

1 English cucumber, seeded and peeled
2 firm tomatoes, seeded and peeled
1 tbsp white wine vinegar
1 tbsp extra virgin olive oil
pinch of salt
2 heaped tbsp finely chopped parsley
freshly ground black pepper

Cut cucumber and tomatoes into
tiny cubes
Toss with vinegar, oil and salt

## To serve

Transfer cooled rice to 200 ml moulds
and press down to compact
Invert onto the centre of individual
serving plates
Spoon Confetti Salad around each
rice mound
Sprinkle with parsley and season with
black pepper

# Leg of Lamb with Pea and Pepper Puffs

2,5 kg leg of lamb
sea salt
freshly ground black pepper
1 tbsp vegetable oil
1 cup apple juice
1 Golden Delicious apple, grated
4 cloves garlic, chopped
1 large onion, chopped
1 tbsp butter
1 glass of dry white wine
leaves of 4 sprigs of fresh thyme
2 tbsp flour

Set oven to 150 °C
Rub leg of lamb with salt and pepper
Heat oil in a pan and brown meat on all sides
Place in an oven dish, and add juice, apple, garlic and onion
Cover and bake in preheated oven for 3½ hours
Remove lamb from dish, cover and let rest
Place oven dish on stovetop, add butter, wine, thyme and flour
Stir over medium heat until sauce thickens
Cut leg of lamb into thin slices, heat in sauce and serve with Pea and Pepper Puffs

## Pea and Pepper Puffs

2 tbsp butter
3 tbsp flour
1¼ cups milk
3 tbsp finely grated parmesan
150 g fresh garden peas or petit pois
4 red bell peppers, roasted, skinned and seeded
2 tbsp finely chopped fresh parsley
sea salt
freshly ground black pepper
2 sheets frozen puff pastry, thawed
1 egg yolk, beaten

Set oven to 180 °C
Heat butter in a saucepan and stir in flour with a whisk
Add about 100 ml milk at a time and stir until thickened
Remove from heat and stir in parmesan, peas, peppers and parsley, then season and let cool
Roll out pastry until doubled in size, cut into twelve 7 cm circles and line twelve small muffin-pan cups
Fill to about two-thirds with pea and pepper mixture, and brush edges of pastry with egg yolk
Cut out twelve smaller circles from the remaining pastry and place on top
Press with a fork to seal edges and pierce once
Bake in preheated oven until golden brown

# Picasso Trifle

1 Vanilla Sour Cream Cake
6 to 8 Red Berry Jellies
Vanilla Cream
marsala or dessert wine
preserved figs, sliced

Use large individual plates
Place 1 thin slice of Vanilla Sour
Cream Cake on each plate
Place 1 Red Berry Jelly on each plate
Spoon a bit of Vanilla Cream onto
each plate
Pour wine into small cups and add
one to each plate
Garnish with fig slices

## Vanilla Sour Cream Cake

½ cup butter, softened at room temperature
½ cup sour cream
1½ cups sugar
5 eggs
pinch of salt
1½ tsp vanilla extract
1½ cups self-raising flour, sifted

Set oven to 170 °C
Grease and line the base of a 22 cm
springform pan
Cream butter, sour cream and sugar
with an electric mixer
Add eggs one at a time, beating well
after each addition
Add salt and vanilla

Turn mixer to lowest speed, and
gradually beat in flour
Pour into pan and bake in preheated
oven for 75 minutes

## Red Berry Jelly

400 g fresh berries
1 tbsp sugar (use more, if preferred)
250 ml cranberry juice
7 tbsp water
4 tsp gelatine

Heat berries and sugar in a saucepan,
and stir until sugar has dissolved
Remove from heat and add juice
Pour water into a small saucepan and
sprinkle gelatine over
Heat slowly until gelatine has
dissolved, and stir into berries
Pour into small glasses and refrigerate
until set

## Vanilla Cream

125 ml fresh cream
1 tsp vanilla extract
3 tsp castor sugar
125 ml mascarpone, softened at
room temperature

Whisk together cream, vanilla and
sugar until soft peaks form
Fold in mascarpone

THE PLATE SYMBOLISES
AN OFFERING OR A
GIFT IT HOLDS THE
FOOD, LOVE, PROTEC-
TION, NOURISHMENT,
SACRIFICE AND CARE A PARENT, LEADER, HOST
OR LOVER OFFERS ANOTHER. THE EVEN-SIDED
CROSS SYMBOLISES A MEETING PLACE, A CROSS-
ING OF PATHS OR A SACRED GATHERING, AN
EVENT OR LOCATION WHERE PEOPLE FEAST,
CELEBRATE, MOURN, REMINISCE OR WORSHIP
TOGETHER. A CROSS INSIDE A CIRCLE SYMBOL-
ISES PROSPERITY AND
A LONG LIFE. IT IS ALSO
THE TRADITIONAL
AND SCIENTIFIC SYMBOL
FOR PLANET EARTH.

# Comfort Me

Ask anybody who knows me what my favourite food on earth is and they will tell you, Grilled Tomato and Onion Sandwiches. I have read a million cookbooks and eaten the creations of brilliant chefs, but none and nothing match the taste of soft tomatoes and onions inside a crisp, grilled sandwich. Too often I arrive at barbeques to find this delicacy murdered with cheese, chutney, bacon, banana or other insanities. This heavenly treat should be made with only sugar, salt and pepper. And LOTS of onions and tomatoes. It should stand for a few hours before being grilled. Then, only then, perfection can be ours.

Other foods bring comfort and joy as well: simple, simple dishes that warm the heart, change the mood and bless the soul. Find them and feed them to the ones you love. Here are a few of the best:

Grilled Tomato and Onion Sandwiches

Curried Broccoli Soup

Lemon Linguine

Sausage and Tomato Simmer

Pear and Walnut Muffins with Honey Foam

# Grilled Tomato and Onion Sandwiches

butter
16 slices white or brown bread
2 red onions, thinly sliced
6 tsp sugar
5 ripe tomatoes, thickly sliced
sea salt
freshly ground black pepper

Butter all the slices of bread
Arrange onion generously on buttered sides of eight of the slices of bread
Sprinkle onion with sugar
Arrange tomato slices on top
Season generously with salt and pepper
Place remaining slices, buttered side down(!), on top
Cover and let stand in a cool place for 2 to 3 hours
Grill in a very hot griddle pan or over a cool fire until crisp on both sides

# Curried Broccoli Soup

2 tbsp vegetable oil
2 cloves garlic, chopped
1 large onion, chopped
4 celery stalks, chopped
1 tsp finely chopped fresh ginger
1 tsp good curry mixture
½ tsp turmeric
1 tbsp sugar
4 cups chicken stock
1 cup white wine
2 cups water
400 g fresh broccoli, broken into florets
50 g tagliatelle, uncooked
sea salt
freshly ground black pepper
fresh coriander leaves

Heat oil in a large saucepan
Add garlic, onion and celery, and stir for a few minutes
Add spices, sugar, stock, wine and water
Boil for 10 minutes
Add broccoli and tagliatelle
Cook until tagliatelle is just tender
Remove from heat and season with salt and pepper
Serve with fresh coriander

# Lemon Linguine

juice of 2 lemons
finely grated zest of 1 lemon
3 tbsp finely grated parmesan
6 tbsp extra virgin olive oil
2 cloves garlic, finely chopped
1 tbsp honey
2 tbsp finely chopped parsley
sea salt
freshly ground black pepper
500 g linguine
extra parmesan for serving

For vinaigrette, combine lemon juice, zest, parmesan, oil, garlic, honey and
parsley in a mixing bowl
Whisk together until thick and smooth
Season with salt and pepper
Cook linguine in lightly salted water until al dente, then drain and
stir in vinaigrette
Transfer to a warmed serving bowl and grate parmesan over
Serve hot or at room temperature

• Variation: Stir in a little black caviar

# Sausage and Tomato Simmer

## Serves 4

1 tbsp vegetable oil

250 g chorizo sausage, cut into slices

400 g small pork or beef sausages

3 cloves garlic, chopped

700 g Italian tomatoes, roughly chopped

1 tsp sugar

⅓ cup red wine

3 tsp roughly chopped fresh parsley

3 tsp roughly chopped fresh basil

4 eggs

sea salt

freshly ground black pepper

extra fresh basil

Heat oil in a large frying pan

Add sausages and brown over medium heat

Remove from pan and set aside

Combine garlic, tomatoes, sugar, wine, parsley and basil in the frying pan, and simmer for 20 minutes

Mix in the sausages

With a spoon, make four wells and break an egg into each

Simmer until whites are just set

Remove from heat, and season with salt and pepper

Garnish with fresh basil and serve immediately

# Pear and Walnut Muffins with Honey Foam

100 g butter, softened
½ cup sugar
2 cups self-raising flour
½ tsp ground cinnamon
2 eggs, beaten
¾ cup low-fat milk
1 cup chopped soft dried pears
1 cup chopped walnuts
125 g brie, cut into 12 pieces

Set oven to 180 °C
Cream butter and sugar in a mixing bowl
Sift in flour and cinnamon, and mix
Mix in eggs and milk
Stir in pears and nuts
Spoon half the batter evenly into 12 lightly greased muffin-pan cups
Place pieces of brie on top
Add rest of batter
Bake in preheated oven for 15 minutes
Serve warm or cold with Honey Foam

## Honey Foam

1 egg white
2 tsp honey
2 tbsp pear liqueur

In a clean bowl, beat egg white until stiff peaks form
In a separate bowl, whisk together the honey and liqueur
Gently fold into egg white

# Life-Savers

Life-savers are all the same, whether on the beach or in the kitchen: they make your mouth water and save your life. They are things that never fail, they live in the back of your mind, in the back of the drawer and in the back of the fridge. They are there when time is short and the need is great. They rescue and satisfy, they never disappoint. You cannot remember when they came into your life, and you cannot imagine ever living without them.

I use my life-savers so often that I sometimes tire of them and have to put them to rest for a few months, even years. I cannot remember when last I served my Chicken and Red Onion Pie or Camembert and Fig Flambé or Garden Pea Risotto or Pesto and Olive Toast – they are all enjoying a well-earned rest. These are currently doing heavy duty:

Tomato Chilli Jam

Pesto Cake

Chicken in White Wine

Kaleidoscope Tarts

# Tomato Chilli Jam

## Makes 2 jars

2 jalapeño chillies, seeded and chopped
1 small red chilli, seeded and chopped
2 onions, chopped
500 g tomatoes, chopped
finely grated zest of 1 lemon
1¼ cups sugar
pinch of salt

Combine ingredients in a saucepan
Cook over medium heat for 12 minutes
Pour into sterilised jars and seal

• Serve with cheese, cold meats, roasted vegetables and on sandwiches

# Pesto Cake

500 g shell pasta
½ quantity of Coriander and Cashew Pesto
¼ cup fresh cream
sea salt
freshly ground black pepper
extra virgin olive oil
parmesan, shaved or finely grated

Set oven to 180 °C
Cook pasta in lightly salted water until al dente, then drain
Stir in pesto and cream
Season to taste
Press into a lightly greased 22 cm springform pan
Bake in preheated oven for 30 minutes
Let cool completely before removing from pan
Cut into slices
Serve warm, drizzled with olive oil and topped with parmesan

## Coriander and Cashew Pesto

30 g fresh coriander
30 g fresh flat-leaf parsley
30 g fresh basil
½ cup cashew nuts
¼ cup pumpkin seeds, roasted
⅓ cup finely grated parmesan
1 clove garlic
½ cup extra virgin olive oil
sea salt
freshly ground black pepper

Combine first seven ingredients in a food processor and mix to a paste
Keep processor running and slowly add olive oil
Season lightly with salt and pepper
Cover and refrigerate until needed

# Chicken in White Wine

3 tbsp flour
1 tsp sea salt
1 tsp freshly ground black pepper
4 chicken breasts
4 chicken thighs
1 tbsp butter
1 tbsp vegetable oil
200 g bacon, chopped
8 medium-sized brown mushrooms, halved
2 onions, quartered
8 sprigs of thyme
1 cup dry white wine
1 cup chicken stock

Set oven to 170 °C
Mix flour, salt and pepper on a plate
Coat chicken with seasoned flour
Heat butter and oil in a large frying pan, and brown chicken for a few minutes
Place chicken in an oven dish
Brown bacon, mushrooms and onions, and add to chicken
Add thyme, wine and stock
Cover and bake in preheated oven for 1 hour
Remove from oven and baste with sauce in the dish
Return to oven and bake uncovered for 10 more minutes

# Kaleidoscope Tarts

## Pastry Shells

1 sheet frozen shortcrust pastry, thawed
2 tbsp sugar

Set oven to 180 °C
Roll out pastry until doubled in size
Cut into 7 cm circles and line 24 small patty-pan or muffin-pan cups
Prick with fork and sprinkle with sugar
Bake in preheated oven for 7 minutes or until golden
Let cool and store in an airtight container

## Filling

250 g soft mascarpone
1 tbsp castor sugar
seeds of ½ vanilla pod
1 tsp finely grated lemon zest

Combine mascarpone, castor sugar, vanilla seeds and zest
Mix well with a spoon, cover and refrigerate

## To serve

Spoon 1 tbsp mascarpone filling into each pastry shell
Top with the following:

- mixed fresh berries
- shaved dark chocolate and preserved ginger
- red and green grapes
- sliced strawberries and pomegranate seeds
- sliced fresh fig and chilli preserve

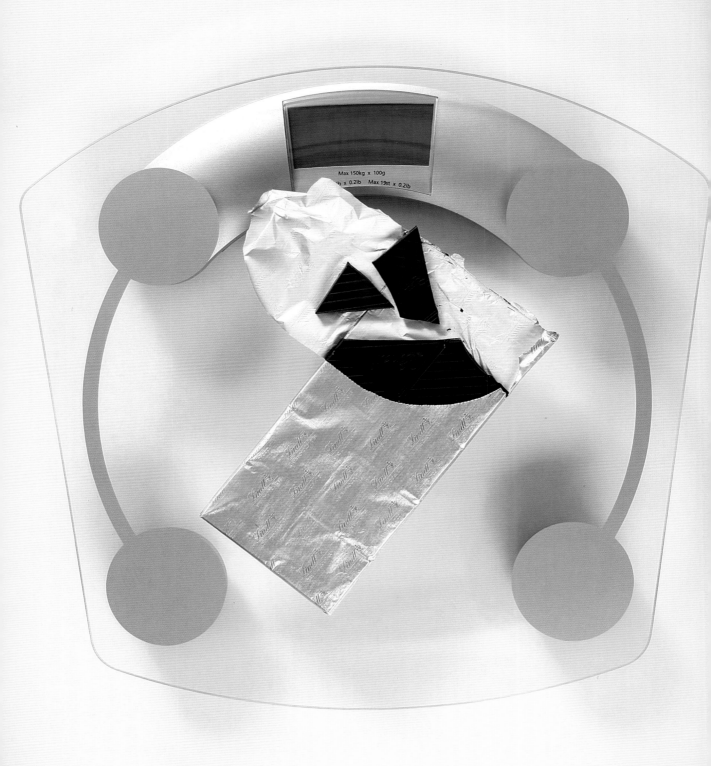

# A Little Less Guilt

Weight gain, heart conditions, cholesterol, ageing, diabetes, cancer, alcoholism, Alzheimer's – life is not easy and life is not fair. There are those born with a fast metabolism; they weigh the same from birth to death. There are those with beautiful hair and perfect jawlines. There are those who chain-smoke for decades and live to be a hundred. And then there are the rest of us.

I spend most of my time on this planet trying to lose weight, exercise more, drink less, detox, look younger, sleep more, feel less guilty. When it comes to food, I consciously try to eat smaller portions, not to combine proteins and starches in all meals, to eat more raw food and drink more water. In previous years these rules would fly out the window when I had to entertain, but lately I find myself looking for dishes that can be enjoyed with guests without ruining a friendship or my health.

The few times I fear a guilt-free dish might be too simple or not attractive enough, I serve it with freshly baked wholegrain bread and a pretty salad or roasted vegetables. These have all received praise from guests:

Vegetable Soup

Fish and Herbs

Chicken in a Bowl

Plums in Orange

# Vegetable Soup

1 medium cabbage, shredded

2 large onions, roughly chopped

2 yellow bell peppers, seeded and cut into strips

400 g ripe tomatoes, roughly chopped

1,5 ℓ water

sea salt

¼ tsp ground cumin

pinch of nutmeg

1 tbsp soy sauce

juice of 1 lemon

200 g fresh asparagus, chopped

1 can red kidney beans, drained

handful of chopped fresh parsley

handful of chopped fresh coriander

freshly ground black pepper

Heat first five ingredients in a large saucepan
Season lightly with salt and boil for 15 minutes
Add cumin, nutmeg, soy sauce, lemon juice and asparagus, and boil
for 10 more minutes
Remove from heat and stir in beans and herbs
Season generously with pepper

# Fish and Herbs

30 g fresh parsley
30 g fresh basil
30 g fresh thyme
1 kg hake or other white fish
½ cup dry white wine
coarse sea salt
2 tsp mixed peppercorns, crushed

Set oven to 180 °C
Place herbs in the centre of a sheet of tinfoil
Place fish on top
Turn up edges of foil and pour wine over fish
Close foil tightly and bake in preheated oven for 30 minutes
Season with salt and pepper

# Chicken in a Bowl

2 tbsp vegetable oil
1 tsp finely chopped fresh ginger
1 clove garlic, finely chopped
800 g deboned chicken breasts, skinned and cut into thin strips
1 tbsp soy sauce
juice of 1 lemon
150 g young green beans, halved lengthwise
100 g carrots, cut into thin strips
fresh coriander leaves

Heat oil in a wok or large frying pan
Add ginger, garlic, chicken strips, soy sauce and lemon juice
Stir-fry over high heat until chicken is cooked and golden brown
Remove chicken, and stir-fry beans and carrots until cooked but still firm
Return chicken to wok or pan and stir through
Serve in bowls, topped with fresh coriander

# Plums in Orange

9 ripe plums, halved and pitted
juice of 1 orange
1 heaped tbsp demerara sugar
zest of 1 orange, cut into thin strips

Set oven to 190 °C
Arrange plum halves in an ovenproof dish
Pour orange juice over
Sprinkle plums with a little sugar
Arrange orange zest on top
Bake in preheated oven for 10 minutes or until sauce has become red and sticky

# Recipe Index

1959 - 2009

This book was published in Human & Rousseau's fiftieth anniversary year.

Published by Human & Rousseau,
an imprint of NB Publishers,
40 Heerengracht, Cape Town

Copyright © 2009 Nataniël House of Music

Cover design: Julia Ayerst at Infestation
Copy editor: Madaleine du Plessis
Proofreader: Marlene Rose
Design and typography: Julia Ayerst at Infestation
Text electronically prepared in 8.5 on 14 pt Vectora Light and
10 on 14 pt Belfast-Xlight
Printed and bound in China through Colorcraft Ltd, Hong Kong

First edition, first impression 2009

Food prepared and styled by Nataniël
Photography by Clinton Lubbe
Reproduction by Infestation

ISBN: 978-0-7981-5114-6

But Frederick, I said,
these people are my friends!
Look at them
(That one? Long story...)
I admit, some I have not chosen,
they simply return, like delightful illnesses
Others have bombarded my soul
Such devotion, such extremes, such impossible demands
A few have even rolled around
in my juicier dreams
But tonight, Frederick, you and me
Let us not dwell on the whys and wherefores
Let us drink with them,
compliment them on their interesting garb
and pluck the feathers from a succulent bird!